ALL ABOUT

Mohandas Gandhi

Todd Outcalt

BLUE
RIVER
PRESS

Indianapolis, Indiana

To Olin, Future Biographer

All About Mohandas Gandhi
Copyright © 2024 Blue River Press

Published by Blue River Press
Indianapolis, Indiana
www.brpressbooks.com

Distributed by Cardinal Publishers Group
A Tom Doherty Company, Inc.
www.cardinalpub.com

All rights reserved under International and Pan-American
Copyright Conventions.

No part of this book may be reproduced, stored in a
database or other retrieval system, or transmitted in any
form, by any means, including mechanical, photocopy,
recording or otherwise, without the prior written
permission of the publisher.

ISBN: 978-1-68157-085-3

Cover Design: David Miles
Original Book Design: Rick Korab, Korab Company Design
Book Formatting: Tessa Schmitt
Cover Artist: Nicole McCormick Santiago
Editor: Tessa Schmitt
Illustrator: Amber Calderon

Printed in the United States of America

10 9 8 7 6 5 4 3 2 1   23 24 25 26 27 28 29 30 31 32

CONTENTS

ALL ABOUT

Mohandas Gandhi

Mohandas Gandhi was one of the most important and influential leaders of the nineteenth and twentieth centuries. His leadership was not the result of his commanding appearance or wealth, but of his strength, character, compassion, and the courage of his convictions.

Gandhi was a humble man who dedicated his life to others—and to the people of India in particular.

Gandhi is best known for leading the people of India toward independence from the British Empire in the 1930s and 1940s, but he accomplished so much more. He impacted the lives of millions around the world with his example and words. His influence was felt by many people—not just those living in his native India.

At the time of his death, Mohandas Gandhi was quite famous, but he was not born into wealth or privilege. He had humble beginnings.

Beginning with the experiences of his childhood and adolescence, Gandhi learned many lessons that would influence and impact his life, and ultimately, change the lives of others. He was always learning and listening to others. When Gandhi was a young man, he dedicated his life to helping others and living a life of service. The people of India began looking to Gandhi to represent their dreams.

Gandhi did not lead from a distance. He participated with people and led by example. When he spoke—often in few words—people listened to his wisdom.

He was born Mohandas Karamchand Gandhi. Near the end of his life, Gandhi was better known as Mahatma, which means "great-souled" in Sanskrit. Others called him the "Father of the Nation" of India.

But how did Gandhi become great-souled?

CHAPTER ONE

Boyhood Lessons

When Mohandas Karamchand Gandhi was born in Porbandar, India on October 2, 1869, the world was a much different place. India was part of the British Empire, and life in the provinces of India was simple. However, most people's lives were impacted by many traditions and practices.

Gandhi learned to write by drawing letters in the dust with his fingertip.

Gandhi's father had been married three times before marrying Gandhi's mother. Thus, Gandhi had many siblings, including his brother Laxmidas (above, left).

Porbandar was located within the small state of Gujarat on the western coast of India. There, young Mohandas grew up with his mother and father. He had two half-sisters from his father's previous marriages, two older brothers named Laxmidas and Karsandas, and one older sister named Raliatbehn. He was the youngest child in his family.

Mohandas noticed how his parents and siblings lived in comparison to others. Because Mohandas's father was a political leader in the province, the family lived in a large house surrounded by many servants.

However, young Mohandas had his struggles. "It was with some difficulty that I got through the multiplication tables," he said. He also recalled playing pranks on other classmates and participating in calling the teacher names.

His mother, in those early years, was largely responsible for changing Mohandas's attitude. The young Gandhi would often accompany his mother, Putlibai, when she visited people in their homes or spoke in the political courts. He noticed that his mother was an educated woman with influence.

Putlibai was also a deeply spiritual woman who prayed every day. Like most of the other families and children Mohandas knew, the Gandhi family practiced the Hindu faith. His mother was deeply devoted to the god Vishnu and often led the family in prayer. She visited the local temple each day.

As the principal religion in India, Hinduism was practiced by about seventy percent of the Indian people while Mohandas was growing up. The Hindu faith impacted many aspects of the culture and

Gandhi was his mother's fourth child. She fondly called him Monia.

traditions of India. Hinduism holds to the belief in a single universal spirit known as Brahman, which can take the form of many gods and goddesses.

Mohandas was a Hindu, like his parents, but he was also exposed to other religions of India, like Islam and Christianity. In fact, Mohandas not only read the Hindu sacred texts, but also read the sacred books of Islam and Christianity. He enjoyed talking to children and adults of other faiths. This early exposure to other religions changed Mohandas's outlook on life.

It created "in me a toleration of all faiths," Mohandas said. He also came to believe that the pursuit of truth would be his sole objective in life and his guiding principle. The pursuit of truth also helped Mohandas to overcome his fear of snakes, ghosts, and the darkness.

Mohandas, as a boy, was neither interested in studies or sports. He spent much of his time talking to friends, or taking long walks in the countryside, or sometimes just sitting in meditation and thought. He enjoyed observing the people around him, and for this reason, may have taken a keen interest in helping those in need.

Mohandas saw much suffering as a boy, but he felt helpless to make any difference in the world.

Although Mohandas was not self-absorbed or conceited, he was, instead, obedient to his parents and he wanted to please them. In Indian society of the time, Mohandas knew that many aspects of his life would be directed by the societal norms and traditions. He was young, but understood how society worked and he did not question the caste system, or his place in the family.

Mohandas was eager for his life to change, but he could not yet see how he could impact the world

Despite the passing of their first child, Mohandas and Kasturbai had four healthy children. Their names were Harilal, Manilal, Ramdas, and Devdas.

around him. But many changes would come quickly once his parents made certain decisions for him.

As Mohandas was approaching his thirteenth birthday, he learned that his parents had arranged for him to be married. This was a common tradition in India at the time, and his young fiancée's name was Kasturbai. Soon after Mohandas and Kasturbai turned thirteen, they were wed.

Mohandas had many fond memories of his

wedding day and his early years of marriage. However, he later remarked that child marriages wasted a family's "time and money." Mohandas did not see how marriage at such a young age benefited anyone. In fact, after Mohandas married, he was required to take a year off from school. The time off put him behind his classmates.

Soon after he returned to school, he began to have other troubles. During his high school days, he ate meat for the first time. Mohandas had always been a vegetarian, and the meat made him ill. Then, when Mohandas was sixteen, his father died. A short time later, he and Kasturbai's first baby died in infancy.

Finally, in 1887, Mohandas graduated from high school. He then had new decisions to make. He began going to college in India, but found the lectures to be too boring or difficult to hold his interest. Soon, a friend suggested that he move to England. He could study law and become a local political leader in India like his father.

Mohandas thought this a good idea. Although he was frightened, he also felt that, in many ways, his life was just beginning.

CHAPTER TWO

Life in London

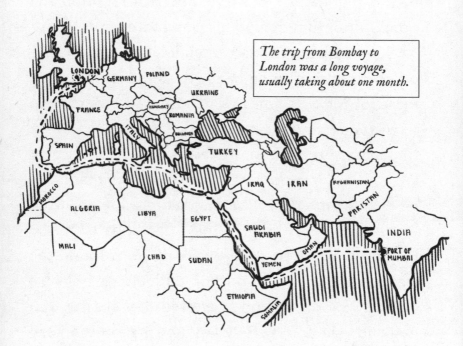

The trip from Bombay to London was a long voyage, usually taking about one month.

When he moved to England, Mohandas Gandhi was forced to leave much behind. His young son who had recently been born stayed in India with Kasturbai.

In many ways, Mohandas admitted he was still becoming a man. He was worried. He knew that he was leaving much behind in India, but he also wondered how he would be received in England. Would his Hindu faith change in a new culture?

Mohandas was still a young man. He was only eighteen years old when he set sail from Bombay's port of Mumbai for London on September 4, 1888. Once in London, he quickly realized that he was in

Although Gandhi was usually shy, he joined groups in London to find friends and community. While the culture was different from his home, he grew to be comfortable with his new home.

a strange land. Everyone dressed differently. The foods and culture of England were unlike those in India, but Mohandas attempted to fit into his new surroundings.

He purchased a fine suit and an assortment of the latest English attire. He also began taking lessons in manners and language so that he could fit into the society and be regarded as an English gentleman. For the first time in his life, Mohandas began reading newspapers. "I had never read newspapers before," he said, "but here I ... succeeded in taking a liking for them."

However, Mohandas realized that his attempts to fit in only made him more frustrated and homesick for India. To make matters worse, before he left India, he had promised his mother and friends that he would not eat meat. However, finding vegetarian food in London proved to be very difficult.

One day, while walking through London, Mohandas found a vegetarian restaurant. There were, indeed, other vegetarians in London! In fact, there was a London Vegetarian Society. Mohandas joined this group and found new friends, along with very tasty food. This group supported Mohandas as he continued his legal studies. More importantly, Mohandas felt that he could continue to be a good Hindu and keep his promises.

All told, Gandhi lived in London for three years as he completed his studies. He passed his bar

Gandhi studied at the Inner Temple in London. The Inner Temple trained and selected barristers within England and Wales.

exams on June 10, 1891.

In addition to completing his legal studies, Mohandas had read widely about other religions. He seemed to especially like Jesus's Sermon on the Mount. He said, "It went straight to my heart." Mohandas decided to learn as much about other religions as he could.

He was struggling to make sense of the traditions and social practices of India as he prepared to return home. In traditional Indian culture, people had been divided for centuries into different social classes. These levels, or castes, determined nearly everything in a person's life.

The Brahmins were the highest caste and were principally religious priests and teachers. Second were Kshatriyas, who were usually royalty or warriors. Third were Vaishyas—the caste that the Gandhi family belonged to—that were typically merchants, farmers, or political leaders. Last were Shudras, which were laborers. Additionally, there was a group of people outside the caste system that the Indian culture regarded as Dalits or "untouchables." The people in that group worked on the streets and

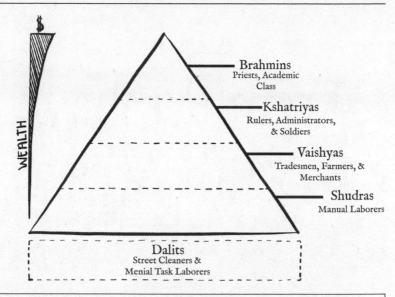

Those in higher castes have more wealths. However, higher castes are also smaller in population. This creates unequal money distribution among Indians as well as discrimination between castes.

cleaned what others left behind.

On the voyage from London to Bombay, Mohandas began to wrestle with this caste system and how it would impact him. Becoming a lawyer had changed him and people's perceptions of him. "It had divided the caste into two camps," he said. "One of which immediately readmitted me, while the other was bent on keeping me out."

As Mohandas neared the harbor in Bombay, he did not know of the other changes that awaited him.

CHAPTER THREE

From Bombay to South Africa

As soon as Mohandas Gandhi stepped off the ship, his brother Laxmidas related some horrible news. He told Mohandas that their mother had died while he was away. "My grief was even greater than over my father's death," he said. "Most of my cherished hopes were shattered."

Mohandas was returning to India as a young lawyer, but he realized that, in many ways, he was beginning a new life in his homeland. Moreover, many of the people in his caste would no longer receive him. He felt as though he were a stranger to the people who had loved him before his journey to England.

Like many Hindus, Mohandas traveled to the sacred Godavari River. Here, by tradition and Hindu practice, he bathed in the river in order to wash away his sins and prepare himself for a new future.

Even then, Mohandas was still learning how to be a husband and a father. "My relations with my wife were still not as I desired," he said. Mohandas was trying to introduce Kasturbai to English traditions and foods. She didn't like them, though.

While Gandhi left for southern Africa, Kasturbai stayed in India with their sons. She raised them with the help of her family until reuniting with Gandhi in southern Africa.

Mohandas was doing about as well in the courtroom as he was at home. In his first court case, he discovered that being a trial lawyer was far more difficult than he had imagined.

"I could think of no question to ask," he said. "I sat down and told the agent that I could not conduct the case." He left the court that day in shame. He knew he needed a change.

Soon after, there was news of a court case in the colony of Transvaal in southern Africa. The merchant from Porbandar working in Transvaal wanted Mohandas to handle his case. Mohandas set out for southern Africa, while his wife and two young sons, Harilal and Manilal, stayed in India. Mohandas left in April of 1893, expecting to stay a year at most.

Southern Africa was made up of two colonies: Cape Colony and the colony of Transvaal. Both colonies were occupied by a large number of Europeans. The European society did not treat non-European people very well, particularly Indians. There, he was judged solely by his race and experienced many forms of racism and injustice.

The case Mohandas was working on was being held in Pretoria, the capital city of Transvaal. Mohandas had to travel from where he lived in Durban in Cape Colony to Pretoria. He had purchased a first-class train ticket for the trip. However, a European man refused to sit next to him. The man called the police and, after some arguing, Mohandas found himself standing alone on the train platform. He experienced this same form of discrimination as he attempted to board a stagecoach to continue his journey.

SOUTHERN AFRICA

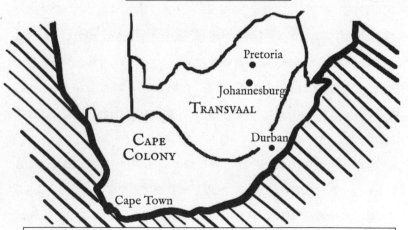

Gandhi experienced discrimination as soon as he arrived in southern Africa. Since he was Indian, he did not have the same travel access, such as where he could sit on a train or stagecoach, as whites.

The Natal Indian Congress (NIC) worked to fight inequalities against Indians in Natal County in the south-eastern portion of Cape Colony. Gandhi (Back row, middle) was one of the founders in 1894.

Once again, Mohandas felt alone and afraid in a strange land. When he finally arrived at his destination, he met with a friend. This friend told Mohandas that he would have to withstand many insults if he was to live in southern Africa.

During his stay in Pretoria, Mohandas again began to question many aspects of the Indian caste system. He also thought about the ways that injustices and racial prejudices were woven into society and religious beliefs. He wanted to make a difference. This was the first time he began to find a way to voice his concerns.

Because there were many people from India living in southern Africa, there was a growing concern among white people in that land. In fact, because Indians outnumbered whites, many laws had been passed in order to limit their rights, giving Indians a

Mohandas Gandhi faced many struggles while practicing law in southern Africa. Once he was even asked to remove his turban in court, which he refused.

second-class status.

Mohandas felt compelled to address these injustices while in southern Africa. He brought Indian people together and shared his ideas regarding how they could improve their lives in southern Africa.

When it came time for Mohandas to return to India, many of his new friends — Hindus, Muslims, and Christians — asked him to help them fight for equality. They begged him, "Please consent to stay, and all will be well."

Mohandas agreed to remain in southern Africa and argue cases for free. He felt that he could not charge for his public work. So, although his wife and children returned to India some months before, he asked them to come back to Cape Colony. He wanted to stay there for a few more years. He wanted to make a difference in the lives of the Indian people in southern Africa.

CHAPTER FOUR

The Early African Years

These were difficult years for the growing Gandhi family. Mohandas and Kasturbai soon had two more sons named Ramdas and Devdas. There was still tension in their home over changes in customs and dress. Mohandas Gandhi felt that his family should adapt to the southern African way of life. Kasturbai wanted to retain the Indian way of life.

Mohandas was often angry with Kasturbai. He did not treat her well and attempted to control her through threats and intimidation. Kasturbai was a strong woman, however, and helped Mohandas to see that his attitude was not making life better for their family. Mohandas realized he needed to change—even as he sought to make changes in society.

Outside of the Gandhi home, there were new tensions developing in southern Africa.

Mohandas was often the target of racial discrimination. There were times when he was pushed, shoved, or kicked for no reason. Nevertheless, he never retaliated. He did not believe in fighting violence with violence. He believed there were more effective means of changing attitudes and society, even if these proved to be more difficult.

In 1899, a war broke out between the Dutch in Transvaal and British in Cape Colony, now known as the Second Boer War. Mohandas brought the Indian community together in Cape Colony to support the British cause. He helped to organize thousands of volunteers who served as ambulance drivers and battlefield medics.

Mohandas believed that if the Indian people demonstrated their loyalty and commitment to the British cause, laws would change. He thought the white minority of southern Africa would make the necessary changes to make Indians equal.

Mohandas's optimism was misplaced. After the war, little changed. The British government refused

The Ambulance Corps tended to the wounded, shared medical supplies, and evacuated the wounded and dead during the Second Boer War.

to acknowledge the contributions of the Indian people and continued to limit Indian rights.

Refusing to give in, Mohandas turned his attention in another direction. In 1903, he organized the publication of a weekly journal called the *Indian Opinion*. Mohandas wrote many articles for the publication that he hoped would shed light upon the British laws. He wanted to expose the discriminatory practices of southern African society, in particular. Being a Hindu, Mohandas also wrote articles that touted the benefits of a vegetarian diet. He included topics such as natural cures and other aspects of daily life that could help the Indian people. Mohandas's financial contributions to the *Indian Opinion* journal kept the publication afloat.

Mohandas also began developing a philosophy of life during this time. Included in his life

GOLDEN NUMBER
OF
"INDIAN OPINION"

SOUVENIR
OF THE
PASSIVE RESISTANCE
MOVEMENT
IN
SOUTHERN AFRICA
1906 – 1914

The Indian Opinion *continued to be published through 1961, almost 60 years after its beginning.*

philosophy were certain observations and beliefs. For example, he believed that "the good of the individual is contained in the good of all." He also noted that all labor has the same value and that everyone should have the opportunity to earn a living from one's work. Additionally, Gandhi believed that a life of labor "is the life worth living."

Mohandas's ideas were shaping a movement in southern Africa. There were increasing numbers of Indians who were eager to adapt Mohandas's ideas. However, as Gandhi explained, "We didn't as yet have a name for this movement."

Gradually, Mohandas created a life philosophy that he called satyagraha. This word, which was a combination of the words satya (truth) and agraha (firmness or force), meant "Truth Force." Mohandas would use the "Truth Force" to help the Indian people in southern Africa. Satyagraha would shape his other decisions and attitudes in the years ahead, as well.

Incorporated into Mohandas's satyagraha philosophy were three key elements. The first was civil disobedience. He had partially adopted the idea from reading some of Henry David Thoreau's work. Thoreau was an American transcendentalist who had written *On Walden Pond*. Gandhi believed that noncooperation was the best way to change unjust laws.

The second element was nonviolence. Mohandas believed that love was a greater force for change than violence.

The third element was living a simple life. Mohandas believed that having an attitude of nonpossession would ultimately lead society toward greater harmony and happiness.

While Mohandas had a philosophy, he had not yet had an opportunity to put it to the test among the larger masses of Indians living in southern Africa. All of that was to change—and quickly.

CHAPTER FIVE

Imprisonment in Southern Africa

In July of 1907, the governments of the two colonies in southern Africa adopted a new set of discriminatory laws that the Indian people called The Black Acts, also known as the Asiatic Registration Act. These laws required all people of Asian descent to register in southern Africa. However, due in large part to Mohandas Gandhi's efforts and the new noncooperation resistance to this law, few Indians complied.

This response angered the governments. During the week of Christmas 1907, hundreds of Indians had to appear before a magistrate to provide answers for their nonparticipation. Most of the Indian leaders, including Mohandas, were subsequently arrested.

Mohandas spoke of this event later in his life. He remembered that there were hundreds of Indians in front of him, including his fellow lawyers. When they were all sentenced, Mohandas was at once arrested and was then quite alone. He was sentenced to two

The Johannesburg Jail was segregated. Gandhi was placed in building four, for black men.

months in prison. He was immediately worried for his family, and he wondered if he would be required to serve the full term.

Mohandas, along with many others, was taken to the Johannesburg jail. Little food was given to the prisoners, and Mohandas could not eat the meat he was given since he was a vegetarian. He was often hungry.

After three weeks of imprisonment in the Johannesburg jail, Mohandas was removed and taken to Pretoria to meet with General Jan Christian Smuts. A proposal was offered to Mohandas. If he would speak to the people and convince them to register voluntarily, the Indian leaders would be released from prison. The government promised that they would seek to repeal The Black Acts.

This was a kind of compromise, but it seemed preferable to imprisonment to Mohandas. He volunteered to be the first to register voluntarily and hoped that others would follow. But his compromise came at a price. Others in the movement regarded his actions as giving in to the government.

Mohandas himself began to wonder if the movement could continue if its leaders were in prison. He hoped that the resistance would only get stronger. The way he saw it, "where there are no leaders, and hence no followers . . . makes not for slackness, but on the other hand intensifies the struggle."

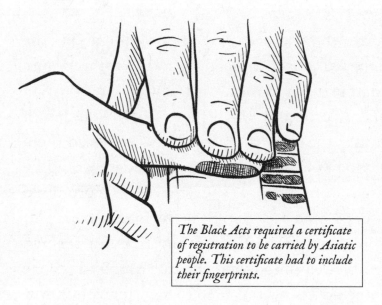

The Black Acts required a certificate of registration to be carried by Asiatic people. This certificate had to include their fingerprints.

Mohandas insisted that he be the first to give his ten fingerprints to the government officials. He noticed that the man fingerprinting him, Mr. Chamney, had tears in his eyes as he blotted

Mohandas's fingers onto the ledger. This display further convinced Mohandas that many white people did not support the government's actions. Not everyone supported racial profiling or the unjust, discriminatory laws. Mohandas saw hope in these tears.

After Mohandas was released from prison and returned to his family, he held out hope that the government would fulfill its promises to repeal The Black Acts. He and the other leaders were quickly

Gandhi and other leaders often organized marches as a nonviolent means of protest to laws that were unjust.

disappointed as the government did not follow through on their promises. New action would be required.

Coming together, Mohandas and other leaders gave the government an ultimatum. If The Black Acts were not repealed and the registrations were not destroyed by August 16, 1908, the Indian people would once again be prepared to go to jail.

The government stood firm. Mohandas and the Indian people of southern Africa formulated a new response to unjust laws. They would march for justice.

CHAPTER SIX

The South African March

During the years when the Indian people were opposing The Black Acts, Mohandas Gandhi had worked hard to bring people together in communes which were called satyagrahis. These communities were comprised of those who followed the satyagraha philosophy. The people in these communities farmed together, ate together, and prayed together. They lived a simple life and sought to live in peace with those around them.

One settlement, near Durban, was quite famous. Mohandas's settlement, Tolstoy Farm, near Johannesburg, was named after the famous Russian writer. Leo Tolstoy taught many of the same principles espoused by Mohandas and the satyagraha movement. Mohandas continued to adapt teachings from many cultures and faiths into his life philosophy. People were learning how to use simple living, peaceful protest, and noncooperation in order to bring about change.

The residents at Tolstoy Farm were allowed to live there freely, but they were expected to handle all the work from cooking to cleaning.

The same year that Tolstoy Farm was founded, 1910, South Africa became its own country. The Transvaal, Cape, Natal, and Orange River colonies were now one country, but the government still discriminated against non-white citizens. By 1913, Indians in South Africa were faced with mounting discrimination and unjust laws. Not only was there a new ban on Asian immigrants, but the government

Gandhi knew that he and others would likely be arrested during their marches. Still, they moved forward, determined to achieve justice and always remain nonviolent.

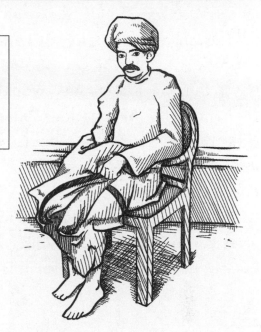

also collected additional taxes from Indian families that remained in South Africa to work in mines or on farms. Additionally, only Christian marriages were recognized as valid. That meant that no Muslim or Hindu marriages, like Mohandas and Kastrubai's, counted to the government.

At various times, Mohandas helped prepare and organize marches and strikes—particularly with miners. Then he would go to the government leaders to try and work out a settlement or compromise before a march.

The longest march, from Charlestown to Tolstoy Farm, was to be a nearly 400-mile trek over eight days. But General Smuts would not meet with Mohandas for negotiations. In subsequent days, other threats were made from Gerneral Smut's side, including "shooting the Indians" and settling the conflict by duel.

Early in the march, Mohandas was once again arrested and removed to Volksrust to stand trial. Luckily, he knew the law, was able to post bail, and

March participants walked close to 25 miles everyday. The march organizers had to plan food and water rations to keep people healthy and fueled.

once again resumed the march that had grown to more than 2,200 people. Hours later, Mohandas was arrested and posted bail again. The following day he was arrested a third time.

At last, the government officials understood that Mohandas was a leader of a groundswell movement. Mohandas understood this, too.

"Government would not like that men should be attracted to jail, nor did they appreciate the fact that prisoners upon their release should carry messages outside," he said. "They therefore decided to take me to a place where no Indian could go and see me."

Mohandas was sent to the jail in Bloemfontein, south of Pretoria. He was the only Indian prisoner there. Weary and alone, he had no idea how the march would turn out and what, if any, changes would be achieved for the Indian people.

CHAPTER SEVEN

Victory in South Africa

While Mohandas Gandhi was in prison, some of the other leaders of the march managed to avoid arrest and complete the journey. They were also sending people abroad to India and England to communicate what was happening in South Africa. Appeals were being made to the British government to intervene in the South African injustices.

The week before Christmas of 1913, Mohandas and his associates were suddenly and without explanation released from prison. Mohandas learned that there had been a commission appointed to look into the matters related to The Blacks Acts and the other unjust laws.

Through conversation and negotiations between General Smuts and Mohandas, an agreement was reached on June 30, 1914. The laws resulting from the meeting became known as the Indian Relief Act and went into effect a few days later.

The new laws had many outcomes. All marriages were legal—whether Christian or not. The tax on indentured laborers was lifted. Indians who were born in South Africa had the same freedom as other races. Indians were free to travel and settle wherever they liked.

Mohandas regarded the Indian Relief Act as a great achievement, but he was ready to return home to India. After a farewell speech, in which Mohandas Gandhi indicated that "he and Mrs. Gandhi were but two out of many instruments" who had worked for change. Mohandas prepared at last for another voyage. He knew he would be leaving South Africa for good.

Mohandas had never anticipated that he would stay so long in South Africa. He had come to that land to settle a legal case, and had stayed for twenty-one years. His children were grown, and he and his wife had aged considerably in the long struggles. They had learned to understand and support each other.

Mohandas was in his mid-forties when he and Kasturbai set sail for India. They were leaving behind many friends but eager to return to the land they knew and loved so well.

Mohandas took everything he learned in South Africa back to India in 1915.

Mohandas Gandhi had changed a land, but he had changed also. He had arrived in South Africa as a young lawyer eager to succeed. He was leaving as a national and well-respected leader who had gained acclaim around the world for his philosophy and determination.

What remained to be seen was whether Mohandas could have an impact in India. He was going home, but he remained uncertain of what he would face in the years ahead.

CHAPTER EIGHT

Return to India

Before returning to India, Mohandas Gandhi's plans were interrupted by World War I. Europe was aflame with death and destruction, and there were new calls for volunteers to help ease the suffering. Hopeful that supporting England would bode well for Indians, Mohandas tried to create an Indian Ambulance Corps. He believed that such a gesture would demonstrate that the Indian people were full and equal participants in society. He wanted the whole of society—and the world—to look beyond race or class or caste. His vision was a true equality under law.

Mohandas's work in England was cut short, however, when he developed pleurisy. Pleurisy happens when the tissue around the lungs gets inflamed and can make it hard to breathe. He set sail for India at last, hoping to bring his ideas of social equality home with him.

In the 1900's, oceanliners allowed the British Empire an easy way to travel to each of its territories, including India. Oceanliners also helped with trading among different countries.

Several communes, like Tolstoy Farm in South Africa, had sprouted up around India. Mohandas himself organized the Satyagraha Ashram in 1915. People were coming together around communal farming, study, and prayer. Others were using spinning wheels—an activity that would become one

More than one million Indian soldiers fought during World War I. Indian Gate in New Delhi, India was created to commemorate the deaths of 84,000 Indian soldiers during the war.

of Mohandas's favorites. Others grew fruit or helped in other ways. Everything was shared.

As before, Mohandas asked everyone in the ashram to submit to a way of life and rules for living. Among these were his ideals expressed as always telling the truth, living by nonviolent means, celibacy, controlling one's appetites, not stealing, supporting local merchants, living without fear, speaking plain language, hard work, and welcoming Dalits (or untouchables).

However, as Mohandas soon realized, even in the ashrams people could not get past the caste system when it came to the communes themselves. Soon after his ashram was established, Mohandas received a letter from the head of a commune informing him that a Dalit family from the lowest Indian caste had applied for admission.

"The ashram had been in existence only a few months when we were put to the test," Mohandas

The Kochrab Ashram was organized by Gandhi. Founded on May 25, 1915, the ashram housed many students learning about Gandhi's ideas.

said. He was elated at the possibility of breaking down further barriers and attitudes in India, but others in the commune were not so certain. "While in South Africa, untouchable friends used to come to my place and live and feed with me. My wife and the other women did not quite relish the thought of admitting an untouchable family back home."

Some people left the ashram in protest. The ashram was on the brink of financial ruin, but soon after, a wealthy businessman from the province came to see Mohandas. He pledged to support the work of the ashram for a year with his financial contributions. This one gesture helped Mohandas to see that people from all castes could work together to change attitudes and influence real social transformation.

Mohandas helped to ease everyone's concerns at the ashram when he met with the leaders and the new family. He asked them to make concessions and treat each other as equals. It was difficult at first for many, but in time they did. The communes demonstrated that even the most traditional barriers and attitudes could be broken down when people learned to love each other.

Mohandas's new ashram was becoming a beacon of hope in India and around the world. Mohandas insisted that people in the ashram be of help to their neighbors. The communes opened schools in the villages nearby, established health clinics, and taught farming to the locals.

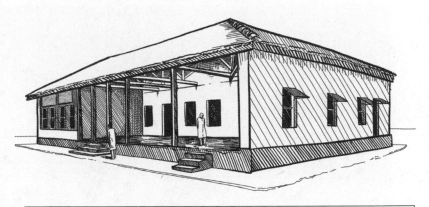

The Sabarmati Ashram was the starting point for Gandhi's famous Salt March. The ashram was originally established in 1915, but relocated to a larger plot of land to help the residents be self-dependent through agriculture.

As in South Africa, when there were unfair labor practices or unjust laws, Mohandas organized the employees and led them in striking against these injustices. Often, these strikes produced results. Sometimes the labor conditions improved, or the government intervened to improve the lives of workers.

As the First World War escalated and Britain was brought deeper into the human suffering, Mohandas made concessions to his belief in nonviolence. He asked the people of India to support the British war

The Indian sodiers that fought in WWI are often considered the forgotten soldiers.

efforts, hoping that this show of support would at last offer India full independence from the British Empire.

To Gandhi, India's independence seemed to be

a logical reward for their war effort. After all, there were many Indian men who fought in the British army against the German Kaiser. In fact, their inclusion in the war effort seemed to turn the tide for the British and their allies.

Unfortunately, Mohandas was disappointed. When the war was over, India was not granted independence and self-rule. Instead, Britain imposed even harsher laws upon the Indian people. In 1919, the Rowlatt Acts were imposed. These acts had made it a crime for any group to organize against

Sidney Rowlatt was a British barrister and judge. He worked to control the independence movement in India and to keep the country under British rule.

the British government. It also made it legal for the government to put people in jail without a trial first.

Mohandas realized that this law was just another form of discrimination. The Rowlatt Acts were specifically designed to keep the Indian people under British law. Britain had no intention of granting India independence.

Gandhi realized that if India were going to obtain these freedoms, new actions would be required—and potentially new dangers.

CHAPTER NINE

Gandhi's Leadership

After Mohandas Gandhi returned to India, people began calling him Mahatma, which means "great-souled." This was a title of great respect, and it drew him into a more prominent role as leader of the Indian people. Essentially, people were looking to him to transform society as he had done in South Africa.

When people in the ashram and beyond began seeking his advice following the Rowlatt Acts, Mohandas called for a nationwide hartal, or work-stoppage, on April 6, 1919. The word of this hartal spread by word of mouth and through the local newspapers. People began to organize.

From the countryside to the cities, the Indian people did not go to work on that day. They wanted to show the British government that the nation could not operate without them. Shops closed. The railroads stopped running. Farms stopped producing. The factories, mills, and mines ground to a halt.

Mohandas also called upon the people to use this hartal as a time for study and prayer. He wanted people to use this time for more than just a break from work. "The time has come when attempts will be made to use labor as a pawn in more ways than one," he said. "Strikes, cessation of work, and hartal are wonderful things no doubt, but it is not difficult to abuse them. Workmen ought to organize themselves." He further commented that the hartal was "a wonderful spectacle."

But the hartal did not go well in all parts of India. While the work stoppage in the countryside was relatively peaceful, many Indians revolted in the cities. Buildings were burned. Transportation was destroyed. In the city of Amritsar, several British men were killed.

While many Indians remained nonviolent during the hartal, Mohandas knew these acts of violence would prove to be problematic to everyone.

The police began to beat Indian people indiscriminately, regardless of whether they were engaging in peaceful protest or not. There was great uncertainty about the future. Mohandas realized that, while it was easier to lead people in an ashram, an entire nation was not willing to submit to the principles of satyagraha. Mohandas had hoped for better outcomes for the people of India, but deep inside, he felt that he shared some of the guilt for the aftermath of violence and bloodshed.

Six days after Mohandas and the leaders had called for the hartal, Colonel Dyer—the British officer in charge of the British troops stationed in India—sent word throughout the country that Indian people could no longer meet together, publicly or privately. But by then there was a movement afoot. The people of India were no longer willing to subject themselves to unjust pronouncements or laws.

On April 13, 1919, the Indian people gathered to celebrate Vaisakhi Day, which was the Hindu New

Year. Several thousand people had come together in the square in Jallianwala Bagh in Amritsar. Some were there to protest the proclamation, but others were making a Hindu pilgrimage.

Vaisakhi Day is celebrated with dancing, fairs, processions, music, and more.

Suddenly, this large group of people were surrounded by government troops sent by British Colonel Dyer. A narrow passage that would have allowed for escape was blocked by ninety soldiers and large vehicles. Dyer then ordered the soldiers to open fire on the gathering. This event became known as the Jallianwala Bagh Massacre.

People attempted to flee, but there was no place to go. The shooting lasted nearly ten minutes and at the end, many people were injured or dead. A British news source at the time reported that 370 people died and 1,100 were wounded. Later, the Indian National Congress reported that there were nearly

Despite their desire to keep control over India, Britain did not agree with Dyer's aggressive act upon the innocent. Colonel Dyer was immediately removed from duty after causing the Jallianwala Bagh Massacre.

After the Jallianwala Bagh Massacre, Gandhi returned his many awards to the British officials in England and South Africa.

1,000 dead and more than 1,500 injured.

This massacre was one of the turning points in the march toward independence.

The massacre horrified the world and filled the Indian people with new determination and resolve. Mohandas was horrified by the bloodshed and stated that, from that time forward, he could no longer remain loyal to the British government. He knew that new tactics and ideas would have to be used to change hearts and minds. He understood that one day hartals would not be enough to change the practices of the British government.

Mohandas began to formulate a new future in his mind. He resolved to bring the nation together. He knew that people would have to be united if they were going to win their independence through nonviolent means. It would take great determination and peaceful protest.

Mohandas gathered other leaders together in 1919 and began to formulate an idea for an independent India. He realized that the Indian people needed their own representatives as well as a form of self-government. They needed to convince the British authorities that independence was the only solution.

Gandhi once said, "The mantra is Do or Die. We shall either free India or die in the attempt; we shall not live to see the perpetuation of our slavery."

Mohandas also understood that the path to independence in India would be quite different than the path he had taken in South Africa. India was a larger land, with more people, and with more at stake. The struggle, therefore, would be greater.

Mohandas was now more experienced and wiser. He understood that change would not come easily,. That independence could not be won with a simple display of power. A nation needed to be birthed. This would be a painful road, but Mohandas was just the person to lead the Indian people to freedom.

CHAPTER TEN

Next Steps

Gandhi once again knew that he would have to lead by example as well as by his words. He set out to inform people of the steps toward independence and began writing about a new nation that could be won through nonviolent noncooperation. Essentially, he urged the Indian people to join in en masse. He would lead, but others would need to follow his example.

There were three ways that Gandhi urged the Indian people to work for change.

First, he asked them to continue to strike and refuse to work.

Secondly, he asked the people to refuse to buy British-made goods.

And third, the people were asked to fast, to refuse to eat, as a sign of their protest and resolve.

There were many reasons why Mohandas asked the people to adopt these new ways of living. But they all had effective outcomes when it came to securing their independence.

Gandhi was easily recognized by the public with his simple clothing. Many were eager to help him and listen to his words of prayer.

For example, the Indian people continued to strike. These strikes disrupted the transportation and communication in the country. The strikes also hurt British profits that were made from the industries that the Indian people supported through their hard labor.

As these industries were disrupted, the British government was making less money and receiving less in tax revenue. They became aware of how much the British government depended upon the multitudes who were being taxed and carrying on the work.

The Indian people also began boycotting British goods—especially British-made cloth. Gandhi himself gave up all of his British-made clothing and began weaving his own simple clothing from thread spun on a spinning wheel. He urged the people to adopt a simple dress, or khadi (which is clothing made from hand-spun cloth).

In fact, spinning his own thread and making his own clothing became one of Gandhi's favorite activities, and people who came to talk to Gandhi frequently sat by him at the spinning wheel while he worked. As the spinning wheel became more widely used across the country, it became a kind of national

The Indian flag features a spinning wheel in its center. Above is an orange stripe and below is a green stripe.

symbol of independence. A picture of a spinning wheel is even at the center of the national flag of India today.

As the Indian people began making their own clothing, the demand for British goods began to dry up. Furthermore, the money that the Indian people were once spending on British goods was now being

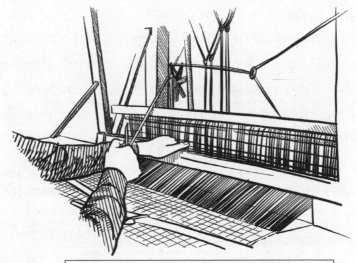

After using a spinning wheel to create thread or yarn, the strings must be woven into large pieces of fabric. The fabric can then be used to make clothes.

used only to buy or sell their own goods. Their money was not going to the British, but all of the economy was now revolving around Indian-made commerce.

Finally, as the Indian people fasted and prayed, their needs became smaller and they became less-dependent upon the British empire to sustain them. They were truly denying themselves and focusing upon an inner strength to win the day.

Gandhi's resolve was greater still. He continued to write about his hope for an independent India. He hoped the British authorities were paying attention.

"I am aware that I have written strongly about the insolent threat that has come from across the seas. But . . . this is a fight to the finish, whether it lasts one month or one year or many months or many years, and whether the representatives of Britain . . . redouble force or whether they do not. I shall only hope and pray that God will give India sufficient humility and sufficient strength to remain nonviolent to the end."

-Mohandas Gandhi, 1922

In 1920, Gandhi became the leader of the Indian National Congress (INC). This body of leaders became a strong political voice for the Indian people. When there were negotiations or headway that could be made with the British government, this body would send representatives to meet with the British authorities.

Mohandas knew that he hadn't seen much of the vast land of India (almost 1.6 million square miles). He had been limited primarily to the larger

The Indian National Congress featured some prominent people in India, including INC founders Gopal Krishna Gohale, Pherozeshah Mehta, W.C. Bonnerjee, A.O. Hume, and Dadabhai Nairoji. The group's first meeting was held in 1885.

cities like Bombay, Delhi, and Calcutta. Much of the Indian population did not live in cities, but struggled in poverty in the countryside. He needed to see the people face-to-face. He understood that if he were to represent all of India, he would need to meet the people where they lived.

Gandhi, gathered up his walking staff and wore his simple khadi and sandals. This is the look that would identify Gandhi and endear him to thousands. He left his wife, Kasturbai, at home and began a long journey across the sub-continent of India.

CHAPTER ELEVEN

Gandhi's March Across India

Mohandas Gandhi's journey through the countryside of India was more than an arduous trek. He intended to meet people from many castes, even dalits, and wanted to discover the real India—especially the places where people were suffering.

On his journey, he witnessed many acts of kindness. He noticed people helping each other and was often extended hospitality. People welcomed him into their homes, or offered him a meal. He also noticed people working long hours and living in small grass huts. There were families which had to tote fresh water over great distances every day. There were other families who barely eked out a living on a small plot of farmland.

Most people had heard of Mohandas, and his fame preceded him. People had come to know him from his simple attire and appearance. Many were surprised when he showed up in their villages, but they were ecstatic to welcome him. In fact, many Indian families would remember the day that he came to see them.

Mohandas was making a special connection with people throughout his journey. Many people were joining the movement toward independence as he explained the challenges that were before them.

During his journey, people began calling Mohandas *Bapu*, which means father. They looked to him as a respected leader. Others treated him like a saint. As he was getting older, his sons also began to take up the same causes that were important to their father.

As Gandhi walked through India, many others joined the movement. Women, especially, were becoming involved in the marches. Thousands of women left towns and villages to participate in the protests and some became local leaders. In addition, there were others who organized marches in various parts of India.

Throughout this time of unrest, Gandhi continued to insist that the marches remain peaceful and nonviolent. He continued to prepare people to remain peaceful even if they were met with resistance or threats from authorities. Nonviolence was vital, he insisted, to the success and work of independence and a just society.

Although Gandhi was by now an older man in

his late 50s, he had no trouble walking throughout India, and he usually walked dozens of miles each day. His simple dress, with sandals and walking staff, became an image that was shared throughout India and around the world. People immediately recognized him and felt drawn to his spirit and his words.

One of Mohandas's sons, Manilal, moved back to South Africa and continued the work that his father had started. Manilal also continued to publish the *Indian Opinion* and led other reforms.

Gandhi's second child, Manilal, was a part of his effort to free India. Manilal took part in the Salt March and was the editor for Indian Opinion *from 1920-1956.*

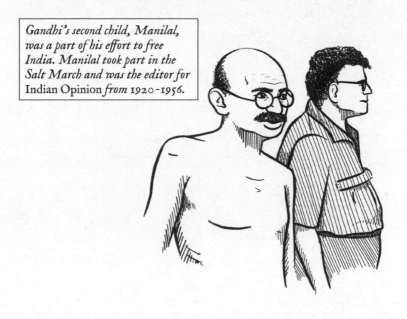

Two other sons, Ramdas and Devdas, worked closely with their father in India and are instrumental in continuing the work on behalf of their father. People not only looked up to Mohandas, but to his sons and Kasturbai. All of them shared in the leadership in some capacity.

But Mohandas's march through the countryside was only the beginning of more important journeys that he would undertake later in his life. There would be other dangers and more important steps.

CHAPTER TWELVE

The Salt March to the Sea

On February 22, 1922, a protest march inspired by Gandhi turned violent. Protesters burned down a police station and ended up killing 22 people. The incident was blamed on Mohandas even though he was not there. By March of 1922, Mohandas Gandhi was arrested for sedition, a much more serious charge than he had previously been accused of. He called off the noncooperation movement to try to prevent more deaths.

During the trial, Mohandas was questioned about many things, especially his attitude toward the British government. He did not feel compelled to lie about his ideas. He explained that he could no longer in good conscience remain a loyal supporter of the British government. He attempted to explain, to the court how the British laws were unfair to the Indian people.

Known as the Great Trial of 1922, Gandhi was tried without legal counsel. He pleaded guilty and requested the maximum penalty.

When the time came for Gandhi to plead his guilt or innocence, Gandhi pleaded guilty to the charges which were brought against him. He noted that he would no longer cooperate with the government and that, even if he went to prison for his views, he was willing to accept the sentence. Gandhi was sentenced to six years at the Yeravda Central prison in Poona.

Gandhi knew that this sentence would be a hardship on his wife, Kasturbai, and the people who loved him. Still, he went willingly to prison. In fact, he saw his sentence as a kind of sacrifice for the good of the people of India. He cherished the idea of being alone and having time for prayer and writing. He was given a spinning wheel, and Gandhi

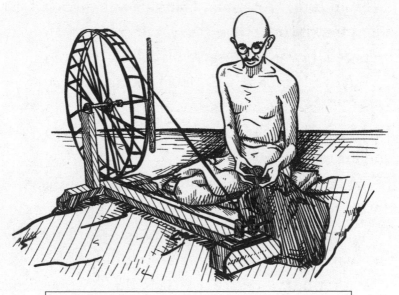

The spinning wheel stretches fabric fibers into string. The string can then be woven into cloth to make clothes.

spent much of his time in prison doing his favorite activity which was spinning his own thread and weaving them into new clothing.

Kasturbai used her husband's imprisonment to rally the people of India. She circulated letters widely through India as a testament to her strength and perseverance. She wanted to encourage people not to give up and continue to make the kinds of sacrifices that Gandhi had taught. Kasturbai would not let Gandhi's imprisonment be forgotten.

From time to time, Gandhi was allowed to entertain visitors while he was in prison. He was prepared, however, to serve his full six-year term.

But in January of 1924, Gandhi had an appendicitis attack that worried the authorities. They rushed Gandhi to a hospital and kept him there until he recovered.

While he was recovering from this attack the British authorities began to review Gandhi's case. They decided that, since Gandhi had served nearly two years and was an old man, he could be released.

Authorities released Gandhi with the understanding that he would no longer lead protests against the government. But as soon as Gandhi was home at the ashram, he continued the work of uniting India. It was not the time to give up.

During the months that Gandhi was in prison, there were other challenges to the nation that were becoming apparent to him. Chief among these was the deepening rift between Hindu and Muslim people. While most people in India remained Hindu, there was a growing number of people who were of the Muslim faith.

Before Gandhi had gone to prison, he had

Kasturbai helped Mohandas in many ways. When he was in prison, she would often take his place in political movements. She also took care of the ashrams she and Mohandas had founded.

managed to gain the support of the majorities of both Hindu and Muslim people in their march toward independence. In fact, both Hindus and Muslims were a part of the INC leadership.

However, after the rise of Mustafa Kemal Ataturk—the Turkish leader who began a broad reformation of Turkey in the years after the first World War—many Muslim people began to pull away from the free India movement, as they feared they would not be fully represented in the new nation.

Gandhi's attempts to keep the Hindu and Muslim people united in their movement was, if anything, heroic—but it did not come without consequences.

In September of 1924, just months after Gandhi was released from prison, he began to fast. He said that he would not eat any food until the Hindus and Muslims stopped fighting each other and learned to live as neighbors in the same land.

There had been for many years growing tension between the Hindu and Muslim people, often with violence and bloodshed. But when the Hindu and Muslim leaders heard of Gandhi's fast, and when he continued to go without food for three weeks, they grew worried. They agreed to put their differences aside and seek peace for the sake of the beloved Bapu. They did not want Gandhi to die. He was so well-respected and loved by all.

On March 12, 1930, Gandhi once again left his ashram and his family behind and began a long march to the sea. He intended to travel to the south of India and arrive at the sea within the month—a nearly 250-mile journey that gained momentum and followers as he walked. Once Gandhi arrived at the water, he planned to break the law by gathering his

During his lifetime, Gandhi fasted many times. Sometimes his fast would last hours; other times, it would last weeks.

own salt along the shore.

Gandhi hoped this journey would accomplish several things. First, he hoped that it would unite the people of India—across castes and religions and economic status. And, provide a great show of unity to the British officials. Gandhi also walked in the hope that the march would be covered widely in the news. It was.

In fact, news reporters from around the world did cover the march and someone named it "The Salt March to the Sea."

Years before, the British Empire had enacted a series of salt taxes. The British had made it illegal for the people of India to make their own salt or to collect salt on the beaches. The salt from India was shipped all over the world, but the Indian people received no revenue or benefits from these exports. Instead they had to pay taxes on the British salt that they could collect or manufacture on their own.

Gandhi believed these taxes were unfair, but that they were also unjust, as they punished the Indian people. Salt was a simple mineral that was abundant on their shores.

As Gandhi walked toward the sea, thousands of people joined him. The small group of seventy-eight people that began the journey swelled to include Hindu and Muslim, young and old, rich and poor, and even untouchables. The walk was powerful—and leaders from around the world were watching to see what would happen.

Gandhi warned the Viceroy Lord Irwin that he would be breaking the Salt Laws 10 days before his march. With no response, Gandhi started his march with thousands following him.

When Gandhi and the multitudes finally arrived at the sea on April 5, 1930, everyone first knelt and prayed on the beach. And then the next morning Gandhi reached down onto the beach and gathered up a small chunk of sea salt in defiance of the law. The multitudes followed Gandhi's lead. They gathered their own salt on the beach and gathered the sea water, allowing it to dry in the sun until it crystallized into salt.

Gandhi was soon arrested, as were thousands of Indians across the nation, for drying their own salt. Many Indians were also beaten by the police.

There was no longer any way for the British authorities to ignore Gandhi's leadership and the powerful impact he was having on the movement toward a free India.

CHAPTER THIRTEEN

The "Quit India" Campaign

While Gandhi and the other leaders languished in jail, leaders from around the world began to demand that the British government address the situation in India. Many demanded the release of Gandhi and the INC leaders.

Eventually, Lord Irwin, the viceroy of India, met with Gandhi and the leaders to reach a truce. He asked Gandhi to end the campaign and call the people back to work. In exchange, the British government was prepared to allow the Indian people to make their own salt.

It was a small victory.

Gandhi requested that the British government begin negotiations with the INC leadership. He was

Viceroy Lord Irwin held Mohandas Gandhi in high regard and respected his nonviolent efforts. However, he was still committed to keeping India under British rule.

sixty-two years old. His goal was to negotiate for a free and independent India. Unfortunatly, the British government believed that the negotiations were merely a formality to keep India as a British colony.

The negotiations were held in London. Gandhi arrived accompanied by this son, Devdas, and wearing his simple khadi and sandals. Between negotiation sessions, Gandhi did not spend his time with the wealthy and powerful. Instead he walked the back streets of London and talked to the poor and the powerless.

Although Gandhi did have tea with the King and Queen of England and there were negotiations for a free India, when Gandhi returned to India he found that nothing had changed. In fact, when Gandhi called upon the people to participate in another noncooperation campaign, he and the other INC leaders, including his wife, Kasturbai, were once again arrested and jailed.

Gandhi announced that he would not eat until the British government agreed to recognize all of the Indian people as equals— including untouchables.

Devdas (left) was the fourth and youngest child of Mohandas (right). He participated in Mohandas' nonviolent protests and was a journalist in India.

When the government realized that Gandhi was growing weaker, they agreed to move Kasturbai to be with her dying husband. They were together in prison.

In 1939, before Gandhi died from starvation, the British government bowed to pressure and released Gandhi and Kasturbai. He ended his hunger strike upon release.

Weeks later, England was swept up in the Second World War. Britain entered the war and recruited Indian soldiers to fight without conferring with the

Gandhi was an avid writer. He wrote almost everyday from letters to political leaders to articles for publication. His writing is described as clear, simple, and precise.

INC. Gandhi did not agree with this approach and began yet another campaign.

Because Gandhi had always been a prolific writer, he once again took up the pen and wrote a draft of a proposal that he called "Quit India" in 1942. He simply wanted Britain to leave India and allow the people to govern themselves. He called upon the people to once again use noncooperation to expose the injustices of the British government.

This time, the people of India responded differently. They were tired of waiting for the British government to act. Many of the Indian people rioted. And the government blamed Gandhi. Again, some of the INC leaders, Kasturbai, and Gandhi were arrested and jailed.

During their imprisonment, Kasturbai became very ill with bronchitis. It was February 22, 1944 when Kasturbai died in Gandhi's arms. She had been in jail for eighteen months. She and Gandhi had endured many trials together and been married for six decades.

Gandhi was growing weaker also. He fell ill with malaria. And in May of 1944 the British officials released Gandhi from jail.

As the Second World War drew to a close in 1945 it was obvious that the world had changed. The British Empire had become unmanageable. It appeared that India might, at last, be moving toward independence.

The Kasturbai Gandhi National Memorial Trust Fund was created after Kasturbai's death. Mohandas requested that this fund be used to help women and young children in India.

CHAPTER FOURTEEN

Last Steps

Soon after the war, England offered India its independence. But a government had to be established. There was disagreement among the British and the Indian people as to how the government, including lands, should be divided.

Gandhi wanted to see a united India, but due to the increased tensions between Hindu and Muslim people, others looked for a way to divide the nation futher. A proposal was offered that would split India along majority lines. The northern region of India, where many Muslims lived, would be called Pakistan. And the Hindu majority would remain in the main portion of India.

It was a difficult time. There were revolts after August of 1946 and many Muslims attacked

Hindus and burned their properties. Days later, many Hindus responded by attacking Muslim villages, killing and burning. Thousands of people were caught up in the violence and bloodshed.

Even though Gandhi visited many of the affected areas, he felt powerfulness to control the outcomes. He was against a divided India, but he had no control over whether it divided or not. Eventually, Gandhi had to accept that Muhammad Ali Jinnah's proposal had been approved and that the Indian subcontinent would be divided along

Muhammad Ali Jinnah (left) is seen as the father of Pakistan, the country he worked hard to create.

religious lines.

In the days following, more than half a million people died. More than 10-12 million non-Muslims (which included Hindus and Sikhs) had to migrate from Pakistan into India. Thousands of Muslims migrated from India to Pakistan.

Gandhi refused to give up on the idea of peace. He spent the day of Independence, August 15, 1947, fasting and spinning thread on his wheel in Calcutta. He led prayer and refused to drink water. He was growing weaker.

Once again, the Hindu and Muslim leaders came together and agreed to end the violence. They did not want to see Gandhi suffer any longer.

Jawaharlal Nehru, one of Gandhi's closest advisors and a member of the INC leaders who had negotiated with Britain, became the Prime Minister of India. Gandhi spent his last days worrying about the future of India. He was almost eighty years old.

Although most of the Indian people regarded Gandhi as a hero and a saint, there was a growing faction of Hindu radicals who blamed Gandhi for the death of thousands of Hindus during the riots.

They were also upset with Gandhi for wanting to establish a state that included Muslims. There was still much anger in the young nation.

Following a meeting with the deputy prime minister of India, Sardar Patel, on January 30, 1948, Gandhi left a dinner to go out and meet a group of supporters. It was a large crowd, and Gandhi was old and weak, and he had to be supported by helpers as he walked.

At one point, as Gandhi approached the crowd in order to speak to them, a radical Hindu named

Gandhi's life had been threatened at prayer meetings previously. Just 10 days before his assassination, a bomb was set off during a prayer.

Nathuram Godse approached Gandhi. Godse bowed to the ground as if to revere Gandhi and then he took out a gun and shot three times into Gandhi's chest.

Gandhi died that evening. There was great sadness across India and around the world as people received news of his death.

Prime Minister Nehru addressed the young nation on the radio and said, in part:

Friends and comrades, the light has gone out of our lives, and there is darkness everywhere. I do not know what to tell you or how to say it. Our beloved leader, Bapu as we called him, the Father of the Nation, is no more. Perhaps I am wrong to say that; nevertheless, we will never see him again, as we have seen him for these many years. We will not run to him for advice and seek solace from him, and that is a terrible blow, not only for me, but for millions and millions in this country.

Gandhi's funeral procession, some days later, was a five-mile long trek, which was only fitting for the man who had walked so many miles for peace, justice, and freedom. Over two million people joined in the funeral procession.

In the Hindu tradition, Gandhi's body was cremated and his ashes were poured into urns and transported throughout India for memorial services among the people. Most of the ashes were immersed in the Sangram, but some of his

Thousands watched the funeral procession for Gandhi. Even though it was only a few miles long, the march took hours to complete.

ashes were also scattered in the Nile River near Jinja, Uganda and there is also an urn containing his remains in the Self-Realization Fellowship Lake Shrine in Los Angeles, California.

Gandhi was a spiritual and political leader, a man of peace, and a man of the people. But he was also misunderstood.

His greatness, as many have suggested, was in the power of his belief and his thought, and most of all, his willingness to embrace those who differed in their opinions. Gandhi will always be regarded as the Father of India and people from around the world, from all religions and walks of life, continue to study his words.

CHAPTER FIFTEEN

Remembering Gandhi

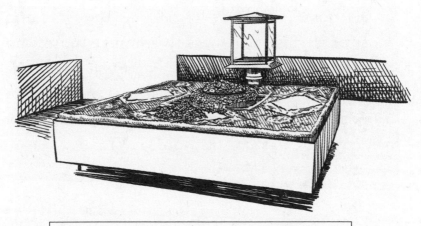

The place where Gandhi was assassinated is now a memorial. An eternal flame burns where he sat at his passing.

Gandhi is remembered as a devout man whose thought and philosophy had a deep impact upon the world—especially South Africa and India. But his influence can be felt elsewhere as well.

One of Gandhi's greatest attributes was his ability to adopt ideas, and to work with people of disparate ideas, across religious and political lines. For example, while Gandhi remained a devout Hindu all of his life—having been influenced and supported by his mother in his early years—he enjoyed learning about other faiths and read widely. He was a lifelong learner.

In addition to influencing others, Gandhi learned from many others who had come before him. William Salter's book, *Ethical Religion*, changed Gandhi's thought in South Africa. And he also adopted ideas about civil disobedience and nonviolence from Henry David Thoreau—an American transcendentalist, and Leo Tolstoy, a Russian philosopher, writer, and social reformer.

Gandhi is also remembered as a man who was able to change his ideas as he learned from his experiences. For example, early in his marriage, Gandhi regarded his wife, Kasturbai, with equal parts jealously and superiority. But as Gandhi grew to understand marriage and Kasturbai, he noticed her remarkable strength. She stood by him, and even suffered with him, in the march for freedom. She also died in his arms in prison.

Gandhi grew to believe that men and women were equal partners in life—with gifts and abilities that needed to be affirmed and not exploited.

There are various statues and memorials for Mohandas Gandhi across the world. Many portray him walking, while others show him in meditation and prayer.

Gandhi would state many times that "a wife is not a slave of the husband, but his comrade, better half, colleague, and friend." Gandhi also believed that women, no less than men, needed the benefit of education if society was to be transformed.

Other aspects of Gandhi's beliefs involved his view of the Indian castes. While he accepted that there were traditional castes in India—and never attempted to eradicate the caste philosophy—he did believe that people should work across castes to improve society. Eventually he believed that people should be free to marry across castes and that society would be changed if people could learn to see others as equals, regardless of their caste, religion, or background.

His opinions on the castes were some of his most controversial in his lifetime and were not widely accepted.

Gandhi measured the effectiveness of every economic system based on the care it offered to the poor, less skilled, and impoverished. He also considered the economic system's ability to empower others to rise to their greatest abilities, even for the wealthy and highly-educated. In other words, his idea of economy was based on the theory that people could care for each other and not victimize each other.

Although Gandhi certainly influenced many

Practicing nonviolence like Gandhi was important to Dr. Martin Luther King Jr. He said that, "The nonviolent resister not only refuses to shoot his opponent but he also refuses to hate him."

people during his lifetime—and his followers were by the tens of thousands—his ideas and philosophy also impacted other people and cultures of later times.

Dr. Martin Luther King Jr., one of the leaders of the civil rights movement in the United States during the 1950s and 1960s, was a great admirer of Gandhi. He adopted his philosophies of noncooperation, nonviolence, and civil disobedience in his marches across the American south.

Likewise, Nelson Mandela, former President of South Africa, was an ardent believer in these philosophies. Gandhi's ideas helped to break the

Apartheid laws and bring about its end in the 1970s in South Africa. Some have even said that Nelson Mandela completed what Gandhi had started in South Africa nearly a century before.

In 1931, physicist Albert Einstein exchanged letters with Gandhi and called him, "a role model for the generations to come."

Although Gandhi did influence many lives—and nations—he remained a humble man and refused to profit financially from his fame.

Harris Majeke, South Africa's ambassador to India, said "While Nelson Mandela (pictured above) is the father of South Africa, Mahatma Gandhi is our grandfather."

During his lifetime, Gandhi was a prolific writer. He not only started two newspapers and edited others, but he wrote many letters to individuals from all walks of life and sent these letters around the world.

He also wrote his autobiography, as well as other

articles and books on vegetarianism, natural cures, religion, philosophy, and social reform. Many of the pieces that Gandhi wrote were immediately placed into the public domain, so that others could reprint them and share them as they liked.

A few years after Gandhi's death, the Indian government published *The Collected Works of Mahatma Gandhi*—one of the largest collections ever produced by and about a single person. As for Gandhi's legacy, he is now remembered all over the world.

The Government of India awarded an annual Gandhi Peace Prize until 2014. The prize recognized individuals who, like Gandhi, continue to work for the eradication of racial discrimination, segregation, and violence. Although Gandhi himself did not receive the Nobel Peace Prize, he was

The Gandhi Peace Prize was created in 1995, on what would have been Gandhi's 125th birthday.

nominated five times between 1937 and 1948, but his legacy for peace is still felt throughout the world.

Likewise, there are statues of Gandhi in various European and Asian nations, and Gandhi's recognition and influence is felt by Hindus, Muslims, Christians, and many other faiths.

Gandhi is remembered in his simplicity, but also in his complexity. He was at once a man of faith, action, and politics but also as a friend to common people. He has inspired many, from political leaders, to religious leaders, and continually worked for the good of humanity and communities throughout the world, regardless of nationality or belief.

Some of Gandhi's words have become enshrined in ways that help to bridge the struggles of the modern world with the complexities of the past. For example, Gandhi always insisted that "good travels as a snail's pace," and that "non-violence is a tree of slow growth." He believed that "goodness must be joined with knowledge, courage, and conviction."

While many in powerful positions continue to look to Gandhi for inspiration and hope, his most notable connection, perhaps, can be found in his friendship among the common people of the world. No matter a person's status or walk of life, anyone learning about Gandhi today can discover a connection to him through his ability to live simply and through his friendship with others.

Albert Einstein once noted these traits. He said of Gandhi, "Generations to come will scarce believe that such a man as this ever in flesh and blood walked upon the earth."

In more recent years, Gandhi's legacy has suffered through many wars, conflicts and bloodshed throughout the world. But his memory has been enshrined in hopeful dialogue and the continuing work for peace—wherever it is found.

There have been many important days and places commemorating Gandhi's lasting work and legacy. Among them, the Mahatma Gandhi Foundation re-enacted the Salt March on the 75th anniversary of that event. This re-enactment in 2005 was internationally recognized and hundreds of people participated in the three day walk. The Prime Minister of India noted Gandhi's influence and issued a commemorative stamp—which is still treasured among collectors.

Later, the National Salt Satyagraha Memorial museum was dedicated in Dandi and opened on January 30, 2019. People from all over the world visit this museum annually and it remains as a shrine to Gandhi's life work and legacy.

But Gandhi's work remains, to this day, an ongoing challenge. The museum in Dandi serves as a reminder that Gandhi's legacy is not a memory of the past, but a hopeful work of the future and for all generations.

In 2007, the United Nations General Assembly declared Gandhi's birthday—October 2—as the "International Day of Nonviolence." And Gandhi's birthday is a national holiday in India.

There is no doubt that in India Gandhi's memory is still revered. There are three Hindu temples dedicated to him and many religious and political leaders continue to reference his ideas and words. Today, people see Gandhi as the one who shaped India into a tolerant, secular democracy.

He is still remembered by young and old alike. A gentle man—a man of peace, love, and hope. A man

who lived simply so that others could simply live.
He truly is the bapu of India.

"There are two days in the year that we cannot do anything: yesterday and tomorrow."

"Keep your thoughts positive, because your thoughts become your words. Keep your words positive because your words become your behavior. Keep your behavior positive because your behavior become your habits. Keep your habits positive because your habits become your values. Keep your values positive because your values become your destiny."

"Strength does not come from winning. When you go through hardships and decide not to surrender, that is strength."

"When I despair, I remember that all through history the way of truth and love has always won. There have been tyrants and murderers and for a time they seem invincible, but in the end, they always fall. Think of it, always."

"To call woman the weaker sex is a libel; it is man's injustice to woman. If by strength is meant brute strength, then, indeed, is woman less brute than man. If by strength is meant moral power, then woman is immeasurably man's superior. Has she not greater intuition, is she not more self-sacrificing, has she not greater powers of endurance, has she not greater courage? Without her, man could not be. If nonviolence is the law of our being, the future is with woman. Who can make a more effective appeal to the heart than woman?"

"The weak can never forgive. Forgiveness is the attribute of the strong."

"You must be the change you wish to see in the world."

"Your future depends on what you do today."

Ambulance corps A group of people whose purpose is to move and serve the injured during war

Apartheid A policy of racial segregation and discrimination against non-Europeans in South Africa

Appendicitis Inflammation of the appendix, causing pain, nausea, vomiting, and, if untreated, death

Arduous Difficult or demanding much effort

Ashram A secluded community or other place of religious retreat

Asiatic A person from Asia

Bar Exam The exam that a lawyer must pass to show understanding of the law and practice law

Barrister A type of lawyer that specializes in advocacy and litigation.

Boycott A planned refusal to deal with someone or something, usually to express disapproval

Bronchitis Inflammation of the bronchial tubes in the lungs

Caste A social structure where one is born into their status and cannot change it. Their profession, religion, and diet may all be dictated by their caste

Celibacy Not marrying or engaging in marital activities

Civil Disobedience The act of noncooperation with certain laws, such as refusing to pay taxes and fines, as a peaceful form of political protest

Communes A community organized for the promotion of common intersts

Comply To follow the rules of another; obedient

Discrimination The act of treating a person or persons differently based on the group or class they are a part of, such as being a part of a particular race or gender

Disparate Different or distinct

En masse As a whole

Eradicate To get rid of completely

Espouse To advocate or support a cause

Groundswell Fast, sudden growth

Fast To refrain from eating and sometimes drinking

Hartal Country-wide work-stoppage as a demonstration of civil disobedience

Indentured Laborer A person required to work without pay for a contracted amount of time

Indiscriminate To do something random

Insolent Disrespectful or rude

Khadi Hand-spun cloth promoted by Gandhi to disempower the British Empire

Languish To grow weak; to exist in miserable condition

Malaria A tropical disease caused by a mosquito bite where the person experiences fevers and chills

Multitudes A great number or mass of people

Noncooperation Refusal to cooperate

Nonpossession Refusal to own possessions

Nonviolence Refusal to use violence

Philosophy The study of the basic ideas about knowledge, truth, right and wrong, religion, and the nature and meaning of life.

Prejudice An opinion formed without or before having enough knowledge to form the opinion

Prolific An abundance of growth and inventiveness

Prominent Widely known

Pronouncements A formal statement of an opinion or judgment

Province A district or division of a country, similar to a state or territory

Sacred Holy; worthy of worship

Sanskrit A language that arose in southern Asia

Satyagraha Policy of political resistance; means Truth Force

Satyagrahis Communes of people practicing Satyagraha

Secular Not religious

Sedition The stirring up of feelings against lawful authority

South Africa The southernmost country in Africa on the tip of the continent

Southern Africa The southern portion of the African continent that spans multiple countries

Stagecoach A horse drawn carriage used in a taxi-like manner

Subcontinent A landmass that is smaller than a continent

Subsequently Coming at a later time

Transcendentalism A movement from the 19th century with a strong belief in the inherent goodness of people, and that people should be truly self-reliant and independent.

Transvaal A province of South Africa from 1910 - 1994

Ultimatum A final offer that usually forces action

Urns A vessel used to contain one's ashes after cremation

Viceroy The governor of a country or province who represents the colonizing country

Vishnu Hindu god of protection, preservation, and enlightenment

Todd Outcalt is a pastor, writer, husband and father. He has written for adults, children, cancer patients, and persons with disabilities. He lives in Brownsburg, Indiana with his wife and enjoys reading, kayaking, and hiking.

REFERENCES

Attenborough, Richard. *Gandhi*. 1996.

Gandhi, Mohandas K., *An Autobiography: The Story of My Experiments with Truth*. Boston, Massachusetts: Beacon Press, 1957.

Jack, Homer A., ed. *The Gandhi Reader*. New York, NY. Grove Press, 1961.

Jhaveri, Vithalbhai. *Mahatma: Life of Gandhi*, 1869-1948.

Lelyveld, Joseph. *Great Soul: Mahatma Gandhi and His Struggle with India*. New York: Alfred A. Knopf, 2011.

FURTHER READING

Gandhi, Arun. Be the Change: A Grandfather Gandhi Story. Atheneum, 2016.

Gandhi, Arun. Grandfather Gandhi. Atheneum, 2014

Gandhi, Arun. The Gift of Anger: And Other Lessons from My Grandfather Mahatma Gandhi. Gallery/Jeter Publishing, 2017.

Kudlinski, Kathleen. Gandhi: Young Nation Builder. Alladin Books, 2006.

McGinty, Alice. Gandhi: A March to the Sea. Two Lions Books, 2013.

Rivera, Sheila. Mohandas Gandhi: A Life of Integrity. Lerner Classroom, 2007.

Eyewitness Gandhi. DK Children, 2014

1869 October 2 Mohandas Karamchand Gandhi is born.

1883 May Mohandas and Kasturbai are married.

1885 Karamchand Gandhi, Mohandas's father, dies.

1887 November Mohandas graduates from a high school in Amedabad.

1888 September Mohandas travels to London to study law.

1888 August 23 Harilal Gandhi is born.

1891 June Mohandas passes his bar exam and becomes a lawyer before heading home to India.

1892 October 28 Manilal Gandhi is born.

1893 April The Gandhi family leaves for South Africa.

1894 Mohandas helps found the Natal Indian Congress.

1897 January 2 Ramdas Gandhi is born.

1899 October Mohandas creates and volunteers with the Natal Indian Ambulance Corps to help those injured in the Boer War.

1900 May 22 Devdas Gandhi is born.

1903 Mohandas begins writing the Indian Opinion.

1904 Mohandas establishes the first ashram

1906 Mohandas is jailed for noncooperation with the Rowland Act.

1906 September 11 Mohandas begins adapting his idea of Satyagraha, or nonviolent protest.

1909 Mohandas's book *Hind Swaraj* is published.

1910 Tolstoy Farm is established near Johannesburg, South Africa.

1915 — 1924

1915 The Gandhi family returns to India, and Mohandas establishes the Satyagraha Ashram.

1917 Mohandas initiates the Champaran agitation, pitting indigo farmers against their landlords and the local British administration.

1919 Mohandas organizes the hartal.

1919 April 13 The Jallianwala Bagh Massacre takes place.

1922 March Mohandas is arrested for sedition and sentenced to six years in prison.

Early 1924 Mohandas is released from prison for an appendicitis operation.

1930 March 12 Mohandas leads the Salt March.

1930 April The Salt March ends at the sea where Mohandas illegally makes his own salt.

1931 Mohandas represents the India National Congress in London.

1942 Mohandas organizes the "Quit India" movement toward independence.

1944 February 22 Kasturbai dies.

1944 May 6 Mohandas is released from prison after suffering a severe malaria attack. The Raj feared that he would cause riots if he died in prison, so he was released.

1947 August 15 India is officially declared independent from the British Empire

1948 January 30 Mohandas Gandhi is assassinated.

1930 — 1948

1869 The first fully-professional baseball team plays its first game.

1872 March 1 Yellowstone National Park is established as the first United States National Park, and the first national park in the world.

1883 September 15 The Bombay Natural History Society is founded in Mumbai, India.

1885 The first skyscraper is built in Chicago.

1888 July *A Study in Scarlet* is published by Sir Arthur Conan Doyle, introducing the character of famed detective Sherlock Holmes.

1888 Jack the Ripper terrifies citizens of London.

1891 Nikola Tesla invents the Tesla coil.

1892 August 9 Thomas Edison patents the two-way telegraph

1894 March Coca-Cola begins selling soda in bottles.

1898 Julia Morgan begins attending the École des Beaux-Arts, allowing women into the prestigious school.

1899 The Second Boer War begins.

1900 The Wonderful Wizard of Oz by L. Rank Baum is published.

1902 The Second Boer War ends.

1909 The National Association for the Advancement of Colored People is founded in New York City.

1915 The first transcontinental phone call is made by Alexander Graham Bell.

1917 The United States enters World War I.

1918 World War I ends with the Treaty of Versailles.

1881 – 1899

1900 – 1910

1919 January The Eighteenth Amendment to the United States Constitution is ratified outlawing alcohol.

1921 The British Empire is at its largest, ruling over one-fourth of the world's population.

1924 The British Empire Exhibition was held as a way to strengthen the bonds between Great Britain and the colonies.

1928 Mickey Mouse is created.

1930 Hostess Twinkies are invented.

1932 May Amelia Earhart makes the first solo, non-stop Trans-Atlantic flight by a woman.

1941 December The United States enters World War II after the Japanese attack Pearl Harbor.

1945 World War II ends.

1947 Jackie Robinson becomes the first African American Major League Baseball player when he signs a contract with the Brooklyn Dodgers.

INDEX

Bloemfontein (South Africa), 37
imprisonment in southern Africa, 27-32
Johannesburg (South Africa), 29
Yeravda Central prison (Poona, India), 73
Jallianwala Bagh Massacre (1919), 53, 54, 55
Johannesburg (South Africa) jail, 29

K
King, Martin Luther, Jr., 98
Kshatriyas (caste), 12, 13

L
laws
  discrimination, 34, 50, 107
  Indian Relief Act, 39
  Rowlatt Acts, 49, 50, 51
lawyer
  becoming, 11
  difficulty as, 16
leadership, 51-58, 80
  life philosophy (satyagraha), 25, 33, 34, 53, 108
London, England, 82
  life in, 8-13
  trip to, 8
  University College, 7, 11
  London Vegetarian Society, 10

M
Mandela, Nelson, 99
marching, 32
  Charlestown to Tolstoy Farm, 36
  India, 66-70
  The Salt March to the Sea 71-80
  South Africa, 33-37
marriages, arranged, 6, 7
meat, avoiding, 10

memorials, 94, 96
Muslims, 75, 76, 87, 89. *See also* Islam

N
Natal Indian Congress (NIC), 18
Nehru, Jawaharlal, 89, 91
newspapers, reading, 10
Nobel Peace Prize, 100
noncooperation, 26, 34, 108
nonpossession, 26, 108
nonviolent resistance, 53, 57, 59, 68, 108

O
On Walden Pond (Thoreau), 26

P
Patel, Sardar, 90
peaceful resistance, 34, 53, 57, 68
pleurisy, 42
politics, 2, 3, 64
Porbandar, India, 1, 2, 16
prayers, 3, 43, 52, 73, 89, 90
prejudice in South Africa, 19, 108
Pretoria, South Africa, 17, 18, 29, 31, 37

Q
"Quit India" Campaign, 81-86

R
racial discrimination. *See* discrimination
racial profiling, 31
religions
  Christianity, 4
  exposure to, 4
  Hinduism, 4, 15, 24, 53, 92
  Islam, 4
resistance
  nonviolent, 54, 58, 60, 70, 108
  peaceful, 34, 53, 57, 69

| 118 |

INDEX

All About... Series

A series for inquisitive young readers

If you liked this book, you may also enjoy:

All About Amelia Earhart*
All About the Appalachian Trail
All About Barack Obama
All About Benjamin Franklin
All About the Bronte Sisters
All About the Everglades
All About Frederick Douglass
All About the Grand Canyon
All About the Great Lakes
All About Helen Keller
All About Julia Morgan
All About Madame C.J. Walker
All About Margaret Hamilton
All About Mariano Rivera
All About Marie Curie
All About Martin Luther King, Jr.*
All About the Moon Landing
All About Roberto Clemente
All About Sir Edmund Hillary
All About Stephen Curry
All About Stephen Hawking
All About Steve Wozniak
All About Winston Churchill
All About Yellowstone.

Also available as an audiobook!

All books are available in print and ebook formats.
Teacher guides and puzzles are available at
www.brpressbooks.com/all-about-teachers-guides/